To:
Uncle Gus
Thanks for
supporting in
Life's Journey

Love
Janice
Green
8/4/10

My Life's Journey

MEMOIR

LATRICE GLEEN

authorHOUSE®

AuthorHouse™
1663 Liberty Drive
Bloomington, IN 47403
www.authorhouse.com
Phone: 1-800-839-8640

First published by AuthorHouse   6/29/2010

ISBN: 978-1-4520-4591-7 (e)
ISBN: 978-1-4520-4590-0 (sc)
ISBN: 978-1-4520-4589-4 (hc)

Library of Congress Control Number: 2010909510

Printed in the United States of America
Bloomington, Indiana

This book is printed on acid-free paper.

Photos by James Dubenion.

My Journey

Inside this book you will read original poetry, letters, and also thoughts that I have written throughout my journey. This is truly the "soul of a woman."

I hope that my journey can help strengthen and encourage readers or becomes a life saver/eye-opener for someone. It was not me who wanted to tell the world about my life; it was God who guided my hands to write and God who opened my heart up to share my story with you! I know I may be judged and talked about, but that's okay, because only God's judgment matters.

This is my journey.
Ms. Latrice N. Gleen

This book is dedicated in loving memory to my grandmother,
LueElla L. Brooks

FORESTVILLE, NY

Precious is this place
the air as fresh as the smell of clean clothes.
The grass is bright green
as I look to my left, I see grapes
growing on vines.

There is not a soul in sight
besides the birds
singing; chirp chirp chirp
as if they were singing praises
while walking into the light.

Peaceful is this place
where two old houses still remain,
But no one lives in them,
a picture, without a frame.

Peaceful is this place
Far away from the city & life
No one on the outside knows of it.

Peace is this place
where my grandparents once lived,
The sounds of nature.
Dirt rocky roads,
Summertime memories
My grandparents and their grandkids.

Missing you!

CONTENTS

MY JOURNEY

(MY PHILOSOPHY)

In life you have to go through journeys. Each journey is a trimester, just like what an expecting mother goes through during pregnancy. Go through my trimesters with me ...

The first trimester is from birth to age thirty. . In this trimester you are just beginning life and learning the meaning of life. You learn life through many trials and errors. This is the stage in your life when what you do will determine how your life will be in the future. This is the time when everything you do matters. This is also the stage in life when you are getting things together and trying to put them in the correct order. At this stage in life you are an adult and are learning to live independently. This is the start of your career; you are either in school or working and planning for your future. You will go through major changes at this point in your life, and you will have to make a lot of life decisions as well. This is the stage when life will seem so hard at times, and you may feel depressed or overwhelmed with life and all the life decisions you have to make.

The second trimester is from ages thirty to sixty. At this stage in life most people are into their careers and taking care of their families. This is the age when everything should be in order. These are supposed to be the good years, and you should be enjoying life to the fullest.

The third trimester is from age sixty until death. This is the last trimester. This is the stage where you should be enjoying retirement and family. I call this the stage where you should say, "Well done," when you consider everything you have accomplished in life, and you should be enjoying children, grandchildren, and great-grandchildren. This is the last stage of life, and you will need love, love, love, and lots of help and encouragement from your family. This is the end of your journey, and God will say, "Well done, my good and faithful servant."

ABOUT ME

(THE AUTHOR)

I am currently thirty-one years old. I am single, with no children, but I plan to adopt. I am a college student majoring in early childhood education with plans to become a teacher or open up my own childcare center. I have been a licensed cosmetologist since 2006. I am currently employed by First Student as a bus driver, with a CDL license since 2006 as well.

I am the youngest girl (baby girl), and my brother is the youngest child. I have five sisters and four brothers.

In my spare time I like to hang with friends and family. I'm also a homebody; I can throw in a movie and pour myself a glass of wine and be okay. I decided to share my life with you because it's a testimony, my testimony.

When I was a child people would always say, "She is so pretty." I heard that so much as a child, and I thought pretty was more than just an image; I believed it was also in the way you carry yourself. I think it was around the seventh grade when I begin to feel unpretty.

To everyone else, I was pretty, a sweet and a good girl. But on the inside, I didn't feel that way.

I always said I was a "special child." I was far from an angel, but nobody knew that but me. Through my life I have dealt with some insecurities. I was skinny and had a big nose and a big forehead. I had a birthmark that was unique; it was all over my body (on the back of my legs and on my chest). My teeth weren't as perfect as I would have liked them to be, and my parents never got me braces. In the eighth grade I was told that I had scoliosis and had to have major back surgery, which made me miss my eighth-grade graduation. I had to wear a body cast the whole summer. That was the worst. Scoliosis is when you have a curvature of the spine. I said to myself, "What else could go wrong with me?" Well, when I got older, I was told that I was not able to have children. It wasn't until after I was separated from my husband that I decided to get checked out (since he had a baby on the way). I went to the doctors, and they told me I had dilated fallopian tubes, which meant that my chances of getting pregnant were slim without getting in-vitro fertilization or tubal surgery. Who has the money to pay for that? Not me, and I would need a donor! This was the most hurtful news, and it caused a lot of crying and depression every Mothers Day, because in my heart I always wanted a child. Still, to this day, people always ask, "When are you going to have a child?" and I say, "Never." But I never tell people the reason why. I always wondered *why me?* At this point in my life I have accepted this, and if one day I decide to go through with the surgery or in-vitro fertilization, then cool; but if not, that's also cool.

It took a lot of growing up to realize that, no matter what or how many flaws I have, that "I am still beautiful, inside and out"! I love Beyoncé's song "Flaws and All"; it is so true! At this point in my life, I am happy being me and trying to be successful and help someone else along the way.

GROWING PAINS

I, Latrice Taylor, was born on February 19, 1979, in Buffalo, New York. Awaiting my arrival was my mother Doris, my father Albert Taylor, and my big sister, Deanna Brooks. Three years later, along came a little brother, Anthony Taylor.

I would say I was a good girl with some issues. My father was very strict and abusive mentally and physically toward the family. I lived at home until the age of sixteen. My life at home started getting bad when I became a teenager. I needed all the privacy in the world, and I didn't have it, thanks to my little brother, I had no big sister at home anymore; she had left home when I was eight years old.

Living at home was very challenging for me. I loved my family, but I lost all respect for my dad at a young age, and after a while I lost respect for my mom as well. I remember as a child that I would say, "I'd rather be poor and fatherless than rich with a family."

Everybody on the outside looking in thought my home life was perfect. I recall one night when my mom, my little brother, and I had to hide in my bedroom closet. My dad would come home so drunk that we literally had to hide from him until he fell asleep. I remember another night when we had to sneak out of the house and catch a cab to go around the corner to my brother's godmother's house. I remember being woken up from my sleep with pajamas on and sneaking out of the house. The next day when we returned my dad was laid out on the floor and in the kitchen were broken dishes everywhere. As a child, I never really understood what was going on; that took me becoming a little older and hearing different stories of things that happened when I was younger. My mom once told me that when I was first born, she, my sister, and I had to go to a shelter for about five days. I can't remember everything from my childhood, but some things I will never forget.

Leaving home and going to live with my sister was the best decision I could have ever made. At home, I was always being punished, and a lot of times it was for no reason. My punishments included no phone calls and no afterschool activities. The phone was my life! On top of that I was not allowed to stay out at night, not even at my sister's house.

My dad was very strict, and my mom never had any type of say about what I could do or couldn't do—all the decisions were made by my dad. I used to be punished for not listening or for my smart (always talking back) mouth. I witnessed a lot as a child. I witnessed my mother being abused and also my brother. I refused to let it happened to me physically, but I did suffer a little bit mentally. How could you witness so much and not be affected? We tried counseling as a family, but that didn't work. I was afraid of my dad for a long time; when he would raise his voice it sent shock waves through me. If I even thought my dad was going to hit me I'd always go for the phone (to call 911).

My little brother used to have welts all over him, and my mom had to Vaseline his body. I had no respect for my dad. I would always wonder why he was so hard on my brother. I wondered if he hated my brother, because it always seemed like whatever my brother did, he would get in trouble for it. Sometimes my dad would just walk by him and hit him for no reason. I hated to see and hear my brother get whoopins'. I would just cry, because there was nothing I could do to protect my little brother. It was really bad, and he used to lock himself in the bathroom to avoid getting a whoopin'. My dad used whatever he could use to beat my brother. My lil brother was my heart, even though he got on my nerves. I used to wish someone would report my dad, but no one on the outside really knew what was going on on the inside. I couldn't tell, and my mom would never say anything. I don't remember at what age it stopped, but I do remember my brother fighting my dad back and hitting him with a football helmet, and all my dad could say was, "That lil' nigga tried to hit me." I couldn't wait to get out of that house; I didn't want to leave my mom and brother, but I had to go. At the age of sixteen there were two incidents that led me to leave home. The first was when my mom and I were sitting on a couch on the upper level of our home. My dad and I were having an argument over me and my friends, and he called me a little bitch during this argument. I will never forget that—to be called a bitch by your father is a hurting feeling. I was furious, so as he was standing at the bottom of the stairs, I took my radio (which he had bought me for my sixteenth birthday) and threw it over the banister

9

at where he was standing on the lower level, hoping it would land on top of his head. My mom tried to prevent me from even having the argument in the first place, but I decided that I couldn't ignore it this time—enough was enough. Needless to say, the radio didn't land on his head, but he proceeded up the stairs. I grabbed the phone and warned him that if he came up the stairs I would call the police on him. He did not come up the stairs; instead he cleaned up the mess. The other time I remember was when my brother and I got into a confrontation and we got in trouble. I was told to go to my room at sixteen years old vs. my thirteen-year-old brother. As I went to my room I began to talk on the phone, only to have my dad disconnect the line. I was mad, and I started punching walls, throwing things, and packing my clothes in a big blue trunk and in garbage bags. I proceeded outside with my clothes and went to the corner to use the pay phone to call my mom. At the time my mom was at work, and I informed her that I was leaving and not coming back. I caught a cab to my sister's house, where my mother would later arrive. I then lived with my sister and my two nephews (at the time) in her extra bedroom for two or three years.

I graduated from Buffalo Traditional High School and Buffalo Vocational Technical School with a two-year certificate in medical/legal office technology; I graduated on the merit roll. High school was so fun. My girls and I used to call ourselves "The crew they love to hate." There were five of us, and we always hung together. We were cheerleaders, and we honestly thought we were the ****. Everyone thought that I would do badly in school and become pregnant once I left home. I guess I proved them wrong!

Moving in with my sister when I was sixteen was the best thing I could have done; I learned responsibility at a young age. I had a job since the age of fifteen; at that time I had to help my sister with some of the bills. She was a single mother raising two kids. I always kept a job no matter what it was or how much it paid. A job was a job. My sister and I had our ups and downs. I wasn't always nice, and I didn't always listen. She kicked me out two times after I had graduated from high school. My mom used to call me a bag lady because I would move from place to place. I lived in so many different places it's not even funny—too many to count. It seemed like every year I was moving. I lived with friends and family numerous times. I would always find my way no matter what, though. I just wanted my own and couldn't follow anybody's rules.

It is with much love that I dedicate these pages to someone who has always been a very important part of my life and who is very special to me: my mom, Doris. This is just a very small way of showing her my appreciation for always taking the time to listen and being able to understand, and for always being there for me without judging me. So often it seems that life is only made up of things to worry about. Life has many disappointments for all of us. I believe that our time here on earth gives us the opportunity to grow. We can experience much personal growth because of all the suffering, worries, and difficulties we have to go through during our lives. It is God's way of helping us become more compassionate, more caring, more loving, and more aware of others' pain. How could we ever dry the tears of others if we had never cried ourselves? I love you, Mom!

MOTHERLY LOVE

My mother's and my relationship was okay. She was not a very affectionate person. We never discussed sex, diseases, pregnancy, or womanhood. I learned everything basically on my own by reading books or getting information from my cousin. I do recall my grandmother teaching me about the birds and the bees. I was in the bathroom one day after I had started menstruating and she busted in to talk to me. I will never forget that; I had no privacy at all.

My mother made some decisions that I did not really respect when I was younger. She tried to do what was right by keeping the family together, which I do understand now; but the home environment was not healthy. I used to call my mother a punk because she never really stood up for herself or for us. I don't know if she wanted people on the outside to know how crazy our family was behind closed doors. I think the reason I am a strong person today is because of what I saw my mother go through. I love my mother dearly and wouldn't trade her for anyone else. My mom and I get along very well, and we talk to each other every day. I think the experiences she's gone through have made her a stronger person.

My mother used to be in the military, and I always wondered why she wouldn't use what she learned in the army against my father.

As I grew older my mom's and my relationship became better.

Finally, my mom is on her own. She was with my dad for thirty-nine years; she then got divorced for two years only to remarry my dad again. That didn't last too long, and she is now separated from my father. I am so proud of my mom for standing on her own two feet and finally enjoying life and doing it with peace. I'm sure it's a struggle when you are used to one person and comfortable with a specific lifestyle, but nothing is worth your peace and peace of mind.

I never could understand what my mom went through when I was younger. I can only relate to what I saw or remember, but I know for a fact that my mother had it rough behind closed doors. She ended up enrolling in the army reserves just for an escape from my dad. At the time I didn't understand why she would leave us with him or with our grandparents for weeks at a time. As a child you never understand what your parents really go through. When my grandmother died, I found a letter that my mom wrote to her. In the letter my mom explained how she loved us and missed us but needed the army to break away, and the army gave her happiness that she didn't have at home. My mom ended up in the army reserves for seven years. The letter brought tears to my eyes, because I never knew what my mom had to go through, and neither did my grandmother. I am so proud of my mom, and this is a salute to her.

SALUTE:

Work, then home,
pick up the basket,
throwing clothes in the washer,
pour in the detergent.
Cooking and cleaning,
Wife and mother,
Hate and Love,
Pain and Joy.
Peace
Hope
Gave all she could give
for us kids.
Gave all she could give
For her country.
At home she was at war
With the enemy,
Light-skinned man
black mustache and beard.

At war she was at peace
with her fellow soldiers.
Left behind flying dishes,
and empty alcohol bottles,
for combat boots,
and green fatigues.
Nights hiding in her home
living in fear.
She wrapped her arms around us,
held us near,
I could feel
the beat of her heart.
A tear landed on my face,
complete silence.
She protected us through our childhood years.
I salute her; she is my Red, White, and Blue.

DADDY'S LITTLE GIRL

My dad—*wow*. Let me just say that in no way, shape, or form am I trying to degrade my dad. I know that my dad does not remember a lot of things, and I also know that he had a drinking problem. I know this for a fact, and it began way before my brother and I were born. A lot has already been said about him. He was a good provider in the home. We always had food, shelter, and clothes on our back; we never wanted for anything. My dad has done a lot of things in his past that have affected a lot of people, and to this day he has never apologized. I don't really respect the person my dad used to be, but I do love him. I will say that whenever I needed to go back home, the door was always open. I recall one time when I wasn't speaking to my dad for about two months, and he still let me come back home. I believe that he cares for all of his children, but he has a funny way of showing it. I believe that my father had a problem with letting me grow up; he has always treated me like a child and does not respect me as a grown woman—maybe because I am the baby girl. We never had any type of daddy/daughter relationship. My father taught me to be tough and to stop crying all the time over everything that didn't go my way. I believe that due to the fact that my father never showed me love, affection, and how a lady is supposed to be treated I looked for these things in other people and places. On Christmas mornings, we would always want our dad to open gifts with us, but he never got up. It was always me, my brother, and my mom. Every gift would say "from Mom and Dad," though. It's the little things that matter the most with kids. My dad was not affectionate at all. No hugs, no kisses, no "I love you." And I've only seen my dad cry once.

My father had ten children (7 outside of my mom): Albert, Tony, Janice, Linda, Anthony, Jackie, Freeman, Sandra (deceased), Michelle (Shell), and me. I did not know about my sister Jackie and my brother Freeman until I was a teenager. My dad had two children he kept a secret from me and my mom for years. The majority of my siblings lived down south (Janice, Sandra [deceased], Tony, Albert, and Linda). I met them when I was thirteen years old. I believe that I may have another brother somewhere in Georgia. I wish I had a better relationship with my siblings on my dad's side. When my half sister Jackie came into the picture, I was twelve years old. I saw my dad show love to her; it was like she was his princess. He bought her a car and treated her the way that I should have been treated (that's what I thought). So even though I loved my sister, I was kind of jealous of the fact that my dad would give her all the attention and love that he never gave us at home. Holidays were holidays when Jackie came around. In a way it was good, because it made us a little closer when she was around and I was allowed to go anywhere I wanted with her. Then, my sister Shell started feeling some kind of way. Shell has always been around; she was the only sister I had known and loved all my life. I felt torn between my two sisters. I always tell people with kids that all your kids should know each other and you should treat each one the same. Kids shouldn't be kept secret, no matter what.

As I became older and reminisced about my childhood, I tried to understand some things. It's hard for me because I still don't understand some things, and maybe I never will. My dad has changed a lot, and it had a lot to do with him no longer drinking. I am happy that God has helped him on his journey and has allowed him to overcome some things.

It's funny how daughters want their dads to be super dads. My friends thought I had the perfect family, with parents, a house, and a dog! Nothing was perfect about it. I don't know what struggles my dad faced growing up or anything about his childhood. I don't know what kind of lifestyle he lived, but I've heard stories. My dad was straight gangster. Everybody used to always say, "Your dad is crazy." He was involved in shoot outs, and I believed he flipped his car over once or twice and still survived. It is by God's grace that he is still here, and I used to question God and ask, "Why?" As a child, I hated my dad, and there were plenty of times when I said, "I wish he was dead." As a child, this is how angry I was. Our family went to counseling briefly, but what good is counseling when the whole truth is not brought out? No good at all.

Now that I am an adult, I just roll with the punches. My dad and I still go at it occasionally. I remember when I turned thirty years old. I had a big party just because my dad said he would attend, but guess what, he didn't make it because we weren't even talking to each other. I think we had stopped talking maybe thirty days prior. No "Happy Birthday" or anything. My dad is much older now, but I believe he is set in his ways. He goes to church, and I try—Lord knows I try—to have a relationship with him, but it's just not as tight as it should be. Recently we went two months without talking to each other. I just pray that whenever we are not talking to each other is not our last time "not talking." I love my dad for being my dad, but some things I will never understand.

BIG SISTER/LITTLE BROTHER

I love my big sister Shell; she is my best friend. Whenever I need her she is there. There have been numerous times when my sister has helped me out. We always look out for each other. Without her I don't know how I would have made it through half of my life. She is such a selfless person. She and I are ten years apart, but it doesn't seem like it. My sister helped me learn about responsibility when I lived with her. She has three boys and was married once, just like me. It is so crazy that after she was married, I got married; after she was divorced, I got divorced. She always was my inspiration to become a licensed cosmetologist. I guess you can call me a copycat. My sister and I are the business owners of "Beautiful Creations Salon." My sister operates the salon; that's been her dream, and she made it come true. I'm so proud of her. Love ya, Shelly

I love my little brother Anthony. He is so funny. He has always thought he was older than me; he thinks he is my dad. When we were younger he used to get on my nerves all the time and stay in my business. He is part of the reason why I was punished so much. My brother and I always disagree, and we never see things eye to eye, but we always hold it down for each other. He is very overprotective of me and sometimes gets on my nerves—he be messing up my pimping game (ha ha). Having a little brother was annoying. We were always fighting, and he always was in my business. I had no privacy with him around, not even at my sixteenth-birthday sleepover. He was right there with me and my friends. He would always tell on me, no matter what it was. My brother has four beautiful kids. There were times when I thought he would not make it, because he was in the streets so hard. I am proud of my little brother. KSP! Love ya, Ant.

BOYS BOYS BOYS

This is going to be a long chapter. I started dealing with boys at the age of thirteen. In this chapter I will be sharing some of my experiences with you—good and bad. The names listed in this chapter have been changed to protect their identity, but they know who they are.

A. **TIMOTHY** (RIP) 1992

Brown-skinned, short, funny, and handsome. Timothy was my first boyfriend. I meet him through my best friend (Javaughn). Tim and I kicked it off real good. He was a good person. I was only thirteen when we were together, so we didn't really do much but talk on the phone all the time, and I would go to his hood after school to chill. He really liked me and was always there for me. While we were together we never were sexually active; we just kissed a couple of times. I recall staying on the phone with him till 6:00 AM, hoping my dad wouldn't find out. Back in those days, I wouldn't go home after school. I would end up in the hood with him and his friends. It was just fun being around them.

After our little relationship we just remained good friends, until eventually, about four years later, we had sex twice. He would always try to get at me, and I would always give him the cold shoulder, until one day I said, "Okay. Why not?" I believed that I should have lost my virginity to him, but it didn't work out that way. After doing the damn thing with him it was so weird because we had become good friends. That didn't hinder the friendship at all; we were still cool.

Unfortunately, my friend was killed in 1998. I remember the day like it was yesterday, It was hard for me to believe; it was the first time I had lost someone so close to me, and it was at such an early age. When he died, I couldn't believe it. I was at work (as a cashier at a grocery store) when I got the news. I immediately went around the way with my boys. It was crazy and unreal. I just remember crying nonstop and drinking. The next day after his death, the boys and I from around the way went in hard. They were all I knew, and I hung out with them all day every day, laughing and joking all the time. To have one person missing was still unreal. We went around spraying "RIP Timothy" on buildings and continued to smoke and drink. One night we went riding around with me as the driver. My one homeboy William said, "Yo, let's ride on L Street." This was the street where the person or persons lived who were supposed to be responsible for my friend's death. It was me, William, and two other people in the car. I remember William saying, "Pull over," and the next thing I knew he was out of the car and I heard gunshots being fired. It happened so fast, and I couldn't believe what was going on. "Bang, bang, bang," was all I heard. The guys in the car kept saying, "Man, come on, get in the car." When he got in the car, he didn't even have the door all the way closed when I pulled off in a panic. "I just was a getaway driver in a shooting"—that's all I kept saying to myself. I thought I was a little gangsta, but not that gangsta. I was so scared. I didn't know if anybody had a description of the car or the plate number. For the next week, I didn't even want to drive because I didn't know what was up. Luckily no one was hurt or outside at the time. After a while they made jokes about it, saying, "Tricey is our getaway driver." I was mad that my friend was gone, but never did I want to be involved in anything like that. These are things that go on in the streets, though.

The day of the funeral, February, 6, 1998, I was only eighteen years old. I remember going to get some flowers and smoking before I attended the funeral. As Timothy lay there in the casket he looked so handsome. I instantly started crying, because all our memories kept replaying in my head over and over. I questioned God as to why—why him out of all people? I honestly believe that he was just in the wrong place at the wrong time. I will always cherish all the special times we shared together.Below is a letter I wrote to him after he died. RIP.

Dear Timothy,

Hey, you know in '92 and '93 we were the best of friends. You were my sweetheart "Lil Trig." The times we shared were so sweet. I remember meeting up at the Delevan Station and the one time you gave me a horseback ride. I remember the time I hurt your feelings and I said sorry so many times until you finally forgave me. You always remained my good friend and always should me love and respect. You were a true friend with no ulterior motives. Chilling with you in the summer of '96–'97 was the best fun. We used to dance outside and act crazy, Every time I hear the song by Ghost Town DJ's—"My Boo"—I think of you. You are my friend forever, and I will always cherish our friendship. I remember when you were stabbed; it made me realize that if you were gone away a lot of people would miss you. You were acting so stubborn in the hospital, not wanting to eat your food. Lol. The block is not the same without you. Every day that goes by I am reminded of you. Nothing can bring you back, and that is what hurts the most. Every step I take—I'll be missing you.

P.S. Remember at the hotel when we were sitting in the bathroom talking to each other with the lights out and everybody thought we were in there doing something? We even slept on the couch together, just on some chill shit … I laughed at you that night because you threw up. Your favorite words for me were, "When you gon' stop frontin?" and my answer was, "One day." Well, that one day is too late. One love, lil Trig.

B. FRANKY. 1993

Light-skinned, short, good hair, and good-looking. I lost my virginity to him at the age of fourteen (November 26, 1993). This boy was fine (back in the day, light-skinned, good-hair boys were in; he was the closest thing I would get to genuine), and he was two years older than me. I told myself I got to get him and I'll be the ****. I was still in a relationship with Tim when I met Frankie. Frankie was the brother of one of Tim and my friends. I told my friend to hook me up with his brother, and one night my girls and I went to his house. We were smoking and drinking (this was the first time I had smoked weed), and next thing I knew he was taking me into his bedroom. I was so nervous, but I didn't want him to know it. So I lay on the bed as he undressed me from the waist down while kissing me on my neck. Things were going on with my body that I had never experienced before. He put on a condom and began pressing up against me and eventually entering inside of me. It hurt a little bit. He continued for a little while longer and then stopped. After that I put my clothes back on. And that was that. Thinking about it now it seems crazy, because that was it. My first time was supposed to be special, but back then I didn't care about it being special. I just wanted to do it. We chilled a little while longer, and then my friends and I left. I didn't talk to him after that for a long time.

Two years later, in 1995, he and I got into a relationship and stayed together on and off for two years. Our relationship was based on sex. I took a lot of stuff from him. He was a drug dealer on the block, so I used to go chill on the block all the time to see him; everybody knew who I was there for. Back in the day that is what we used to do. This boy played me so hard; he used me for sex and money, and I just was caught up in something that I thought was love at the time. All my friends used to tell me to stop messing with him, but I didn't listen. I would do anything to be with him. I slept in crack houses with him; not the kind you are probably thinking of—just a regular house, but the person who lived there was a crack user. I even got kicked out of my house with my sister just to be with him. Here is one story that shows what that period was like: One night I was supposed to be spending the night at my friend Tamara's house, and she was supposed to be at my house. We walked all the way around the block from her house and caught a cab to the west side. I was the main one who wanted to go see my dude. Well, needless to say, I got busted. Back in those days, we had pagers and not cell phones. My mom had paged me, and I called her back from the lady's house where I was, a drug user's home. When I called, she asked, "Where are you?" and I replied "Tamara's house." Her immediate response was, "This is not Tamara's number on the caller ID." How stupid I was. I had totally forgotten all about caller ID. I was speechless, and the next thing I knew my mom and my sister were blowing up this lady's phone. I ignored a few calls, and then I finally talked to my sister. She wanted to know where I was, and I would not tell her. She then told me to come home, and I refused. She threatened me and said if I didn't come home she would have my stuff out on the porch in the morning. I didn't believe her, and at the time I didn't care. I just wanted to spend the night with my dude. Needless to say, I was kicked out and all my stuff was on the porch when I went home. I believe the next two days I chilled with him and then ended up living with Tamara for a few days until I moved in with my sister (Jackie) and her boyfriend.

I stopped messing with Franky when he became abusive and an alcoholic. The first time he punched me was on the block in front of everybody. It came out of nowhere. Boom, right in the jaw—I was in shock! I was sitting in the car with three other guys, about to drop them off. He had lost his money gambling, so he wanted them to give me gas money so I could give it to him. We in the car clowning around, and they were telling me to just pull off. But I had my dude in my ear saying, "You'd better not move this car until they give you some money," and that's when he punched me as I was sitting in the driver's seat. I backed up and started kicking him through the window and then got out of the car, and he yoked me up. His boys grabbed him, and I got in the car and drove off. His brother (who was in the car) told me to leave him alone. But I didn't listen, and I went back to where he was. He apologized, and we stayed the night together only to get into another fight. This time he had me on the floor in my own house, unplugged the phone, and kicked me out of my own bed. I went across the street and called my friend Tamara on the pay phone and told her what was going on. I cried and cried until I fell asleep on the couch. I became scared of him, because this was a side of him I had never seen before. The next morning he got up and left without saying anything to me. He called and told me not to come up to the block anymore. So I didn't for about a month. And when I did go it was with my friends, and I would sit my ass right in the car with the windows rolled up until one day he was up there and told me to get out. We talked and continued seeing each other, and everything seemed cool until I got hit two more times in our relationship, and I said enough is enough. I kept saying to myself, "I am not that bitch to be getting abused." I believed he could not control his alcohol or his hands, and I refused to be a punching bag. I told him I couldn't mess with him after I found out he was messing with another girl. That was my only escape; I needed another reason. I was through trying to fight over him and everything else. I just couldn't do it anymore. I never messed with him again, but I would occasionally over the years speak with him. Later he apologized and stated that he realized that he had messed up a good thing and that I was a good girl. He still tried to get back with me. I decided to leave the past in the past. Back in the day I thought I'd never stop messing with him, and I actually thought that I was in love. But as I got older and wiser I realized that it never was love. The last I heard he still has a gambling and drinking problem.

C. MITCHELL, JULY 19, 1995

Pretty brown eyes. I dated him for six months at the age of fifteen. His brother lived down the street from me. There wasn't too much I knew about dating at this age. I remember that in the summertime we used to ride our bikes together, and I skipped school with him twice. In this relationship I experienced the meaning of an "STD." We had an okay relationship. Back then everything was based on sex. There was no love thing (at least not with me). I caught chlamydia from him and did not tell anyone, not even him. The sex was good, and his penis was huge. I experienced sex up against the wall, and that was the bomb. But for all this good sex I paid a price. What always looks and feels good is not always good.

One day I wasn't feeling so right down there, so I made a appointment with my GYN, and when I went they informed me that I had a yeast infection and gave me a prescription, I took the prescription and still had the same problem. When I went back they discovered I had chlamydia, and nobody knew I was having sex, so I couldn't tell anyone in my family, not even my sister. The funny part about this is that my mom took me to both appointments and even got my prescription filled and she didn't even know. I couldn't let anyone find out. I was only fifteen years old. I knew about STDs, but I never thought I'd catch one. Condoms weren't advertised back then as much as they are now, nor was HIV/AIDS as big an issue as it is now; but it was around. When I found out I had an STD I didn't cry at first—until I started thinking. I couldn't believe this nasty nigga had given me something. And where did *he* get it? This could have been HIV/AIDS or something I couldn't get rid of. I stopped all sexual contact with this guy and didn't give him a reason why, and he kept trying to get with me. After a year I told him why I stopped messing with him; he just denied it and still wanted to be with me after that! I couldn't believe him.

D. RAY 1998

Brown-skinned, with a job and a car. Okay, let's try again. I'm eighteen years old now. Ray was cool. He had a car and a job, and we did things together—we went on dates. We went bowling together, and skating, and we just had fun together. I was finally "a winner." We talked all the time, and at this time I was living with roommates, so he used to come and stay the night with me at least three or four times a week. Everything was good for the first five months, and then he started becoming distant. My pages weren't being returned, and he wasn't calling me as much or coming over as often. Our communication wasn't the same, but we were still supposed to be in a relationship. I remember that one day I was on my way to work in my dad's car, and my dad kicked me out of his car. I called Ray, crying, and he came right away to pick me up and take me home.

One day the girls and I were sitting around having discussions about miscarriages, birth control pills, pregnancy, and just girly stuff. In the conversation we were saying that you have spotting when you have a miscarriage. I had some spotting in my panties around the time, but I knew I wasn't pregnant. So I went and got a clean pair and showed them, because the stains were still on them after I had washed them. My friend said, "You got crabs, and

41

them little dots is blood." I felt so nasty. I had read about these nasty things, but again I thought it couldn't happen to me. No condom could have prevented this, so either way I lost again. My friend and I went to the drugstore and got the medicine. When I returned home and got in the shower I cried and cried and cried, and when I saw them on my rag I screamed; this was the worst thing ever. If you have never had crabs you are blessed. They are so nasty. I had to shave all my hair and wash and dry all my sheets and clothes, because if you don't do this and one is left behind that one can lay more eggs. I keep blaming myself over and over, but there was nothing I could have done to prevent it, besides practice abstinence. I told Ray about this, and again I received the famous answer "I don't have anything," which I knew was a lie because I was told that someone saw him in the drugstore one day picking up something—he said it was medicine for his grandmother. We had an open discussion about this, and because it's not an STD I just blamed it on the house; we had people in and out all the time. I couldn't really pinpoint anything because it's not an STD and people kept saying, "You can get them from anywhere," which is true. But I know that he gave them to me. Everything from there went downhill because I had a trust issue now. I thought I had someone real; we had more than just sex in that relationship.

Later on in the relationship I found out through one of his friends that he was cheating on me with someone else. I knew who this girl was from skating, and I also found out that another girl was pregnant by him around this same time. One night I saw him in traffic with the girl in the car (not the pregnant one), and I followed him to his house. He told the girl to go in the house as we talked outside. He claimed she was just a friend, and I'm like, "Okay, why is she coming to your house?" I later spoke to the girl, and she said she didn't know about me but that they were just friends. She said she was not in a relationship with him, nor did she want one, but they had been sexually involved. So we start putting two and two together; you know how we girls do. Pull out the calendars and let's check some dates. It's one thing to be cheated on, but it's another thing when you are being cheated on and the nigga is not using any protection. I remember one time I thought I might have been pregnant by him, and I kept saying, "If I am, I'm keeping it." After all the drama, I immediately stopped all contact with him and went away to Cleveland for two weeks, but before I left I wrote him a four-page letter. It was a nice letter too.

Like they all do, he apologized for hurting me and said he still loved me and wanted me back. As much as my heart wanted to go back to him, I couldn't do it to myself again. I usually don't hold grudges against people. I just take it as a learning experience and keep moving. I still speak to him when I see him, because over all he was a nice guy, with a great personality.

LOVE

September 1998–

Finally, love had found me and stayed with me for more than five years. After the relationship with Ray I said that I was finished with these guys for a while, but someone else said no—not yet! One guy I had known from the neighborhood was a good friend. He was in a singing group called "Off the Block." I never knew he had any feelings for me or was interested in me in any type of way. He lived in New Jersey at the time, trying to pursue a music career, and when he came home he was looking for me. I was living back at home with my father, and my neighbor said, "Allen came by looking for you," and I said "Why is he looking for me?" One night I was sitting on my porch and he came by with his friend (Mario). We all sat in front of my house talking, and he said he'd be back. He came back by himself, and as we talked he expressed his feeling for me and told me that he had dreams about me and that he was always thinking about me and didn't know where the feelings are coming from, but he knew that they are real. I had already been told by Mario that Allen liked me, but I just acted like I didn't know. We sat on my porch and talked for about an hour. We discussed his career and how I had just gotten out of a relationship and was not trying to jump into another relationship because I had been hurt so many times. We discussed love, life, and the future. That same week he had to go back to New Jersey, and we continued in contact with each other, writing each other back and forth.

Sex never became an issue in our conversation or letters. When he came to Buffalo again we went on our first little date (to our special place), and it was so sweet; we just sat looking at the water as he held me. I felt so safe in his arms, like a baby being held for the first time. We took it slow in the beginning. Every time he was home we were together. The first night we spent together he held me all night; this was a feeling I can't explain. He never touched me in a sexual way or forced anything on me. The first time we kissed we danced together; we danced in the middle of the living room to Usher and Monica's song "Slow Jam." It was like a fairy tale to me. I knew this guy, but I never knew he was so sweet and smooth. The first time we made love it was so passionate. He asked me two times if I was sure I was ready. He was such a gentlemen in bed; it wasn't just about him—it was about us. I stayed with him that night, and the next day and night we stayed on Bissell in a friend's house by ourselves. When I woke up the next morning he had bath water run for me and a candle lit, and he washed my back and gave me a massage. I felt like I was in heaven. He also used to sing to me. I knew he could sing his ass off, but he was singing to me. I remember kissing on Bissell, and Mario took a picture of us kissing. Our relationship started on September 6, 1998, and by Thanksgiving 1998, we were living together. It was not planned that we would live together. My friend and I had gotten an apartment together in October, and they were having some problems in New Jersey at the time, so he and his singing partner (Mario) came to stay with us. Our love grew even stronger for each other. I met his family, he met mine, and we were doing family dinners together. I was accepted by his family, and he was accepted by mine. Our nieces and nephews referred to us as Aunty Tricey and Uncle Allen.

During the relationship there were some challenging times. I dealt with the females he associated with, and he dealt with my ex-boyfriends. During the first three years of our relationship we broke up twice, but the breakups never lasted more than one or two weeks. We always overcame the obstacles because we were in love and we were the perfect couple, All our friends looked at our relationship as something so pure and real.

Everything on the outside looked so sweet, but in any relationship you are going to go through some problems, and we were still young. We were only nineteen and twenty when we started living together.

I had to deal with a girl from New Jersey (I call her psycho) who loved Allen. She and Allen had sex once before we became a couple and—let him tell it—he says, "She's just sprung; she's crazy." This girl lived in the same house with him and his friends. She was the live-in babysitter for his manager (at the time). I recall going to New Jersey to visit him, and I stayed for two weeks in this house. She was kind of wary about me being there, but all she could do was respect the fact that I was his girlfriend; not her. The first week I was there, the animosity between us was crazy. Allen had to check her once. I didn't speak to her at all; I was there for him, not her. We almost got into a fight once in the house; then about the last week I was there we were speaking, but it was time for me to bounce. Allen's manager (at the time) was trying to get me to stay and get a job there. If she wasn't there I would have, but the fact that they were once involved didn't sit well with me.

After I returned to Buffalo I used to argue with this girl over the phone, because she still didn't get it. She became a prostitute while living in New Jersey, so she used to give Allen money and buy him things, and of course he accepted everything from her. I was tired of it, and I was tired of her. Well, I had to let off some steam, so one weekend when she came to Buffalo and I found out she was here I went to fight her. It's funny, because I fought her in Allen's sister's house. That wasn't the plan. I was supposed to meet Allen's sister out at the club and fight her there. I couldn't wait when I found out that Allen was over there, which made me more upset. I called him on the phone and heard her in the background, so my friend Moe and I walked in the cold for about fifteen minutes to get my sister's car and headed to Allen's sister's house. As soon as he saw me pull up, he went walking off down the street, not even turning around. I walked upstairs, and all eyes were on me in shock, I told Allen's little brother to take my baby nephew downstairs, and that was it—the girl and I started beefing. She was sitting down on a chair, and when she looked up, there was no time for any reaction. It was beef on sight. I went crazy. I was kicking and punching until she grabbed hold of my hair; the bitch wouldn't let up at all. At this point in time, I didn't care about my hair, but I wanted to get at her a little bit more. I ended up on the floor, and that was it. She wouldn't let up, and there was nothing more I could do. Allen's mother lived downstairs and heard all the commotion upstairs, not knowing that this girl was over there. She came upstairs and broke up the fight and told her to leave and that I was Allen's girlfriend and her daughter-in-law and that she had no business even coming to the house.

Allen decided to come back to the house after the fight was over, as if he didn't know what was going on. At this point in time, Allen and I almost got into a fight. The girl got into a cab and left, and later that night I went to a bar to get Allen's other sister (who was waiting for me at the bar). While we were talking in the car, Allen and Mario rode up. Mario was hot, and Allen jumped into my car and Moe and Mario left. I was so done with him; I wanted him to get all his things and just leave. We sat in the car for an hour just talking with his sister, and he decided to stay with me and work it out, which meant not communicating or accepting anything from the girl. That lasted for about a year. One night I just lost my mind when I heard her on his voice mail. He was about to go to New York for the weekend for music, but she was on his voice mail trying to find out when he would be there. We got into a big fight, and I told him that if he went he couldn't come back and it was over. I mean, this was the worst fight we had ever been through. This was the end for me; I couldn't take it anymore. We cried, and he didn't leave. I made him call her and tell her that he couldn't talk to her anymore. He refused to do it at first because he was concerned that she would hurt herself. I didn't care about her or her life at this time, so I said, "You are putting her first over our relationship." I said, "I have no pity for that *****; she doesn't respect me or our relationship." She still kept after him after the fight. He made the call, and she didn't answer. He made another call—no answer, I suggested he leave a message, but he said she would just say she never got it, and he would rather speak directly to her. We tried two more times and never got an answer. Needless to say the call was never made. I didn't deal with her anymore for a while. I had decided to just focus on my relationship with Allen.

After three years and four months together we decided, after marriage counseling, to get married. We had a good relationship, we loved each other, we overcame all the bad times, and we always said we would be together forever.

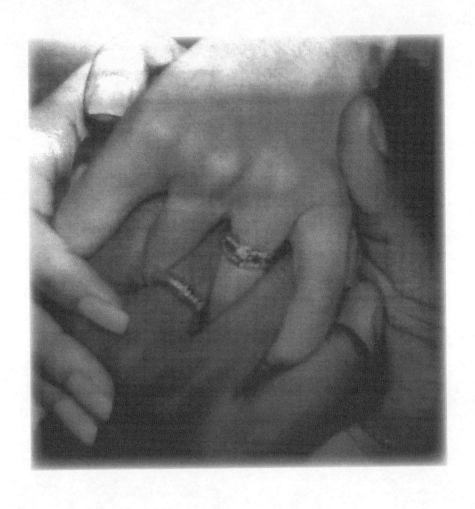

MARRIAGE

On February 23, 2002, Latrice and Allen became Mr. and Mrs. Gleen. The wedding was beautiful, with thirty or forty guests. We tried to keep it simple. We decided to get married and do the right thing. Since we both believed in God, why not let God honor our marriage? We never thought we could live without each other, so we made that *big* step.

I felt so much better at home and not guilty in church just knowing that we did the right thing. When we slept in the bed together I felt so happy and at peace with my baby. Marriage is a beautiful thing, and being a wife was a blessing and also a lot of work. You have to be selfless, and I had to learn that. You have to be a really wise woman to be a wife. I was not the perfect wife. I didn't cook every day or wash clothes every week or iron all my husband's clothes for the week. The first year of the marriage was kind of learning the whole meaning of marriage and how I was supposed to treat my husband and how I was supposed to act as a wife. Even though we had lived together before, there was a big difference. I had to watch what I said, what I did, and how I said things. I had a problem with my words; I disrespected my husband verbally at times, and I called him every name in the book. I'd throw things at him when I was mad.

I recall one incident when he was late bringing me something to eat. I was starving, and he kept saying he was on his way. That took about an hour, and as soon as he walked through the door and handed me my food, I just snapped. I was drinking some pop, and the next thing I knew the glass was headed for his head. He looked at me in disbelief and went in our bedroom and locked me out. After that I felt very bad. I cried as I lay on the couch until I feel asleep. We went through a lot; one time we had to call our parents to come to our house to try to solve a problem. I locked him out of the house in the hallway with just his boxers on one night and threw his phone out the window.

I do regret some things I said and some of my actions, because that's not how a wife was supposed to act. But I would just get angry when things didn't go my way or when I felt that he wasn't treating me like his queen (wife). I was not perfect, but I did learn a lot from my mistakes as a wife. I also became more sensitive about the way he treated me; for example, the cell phone, him being gone too long, him not calling home, him being out with the guys and him talking to females, and of course the music business. I felt I should always come first, and I wasn't always first.

The first six months of the marriage were beautiful. We moved into a new house, and it was like starting fresh in a new environment.

During the seventh month of the marriage I found something that disturbed me—a cell phone bill with a New Jersey and a Buffalo number. The numbers were all over the bill at all times of the day and night. I called the Buffalo number back; I already knew the New Jersey number. When I called, a female answered, and she and I had words with each other. She continued to say, "He's just my friend," and I'm thinking that friends don't talk this much, and I know almost all his friends. I just started thinking, where am I when these calls are being made? I ended the conversation with her and just got into my bed and cried. All day and night I cried in disbelief. I was just disgusted. I felt like I didn't really know my husband. I felt like he had another lifestyle outside of me. Allen was in New York at the time, and I called my friend Tysha over that Sunday morning before she went to church. She talked to me and was just my support in the situation. Tysha was my "let's ride" friend, it's whatever, anybody trespassing can get it! As soon as he came home it was World War III. Of course he denied that anything was going on with this girl and said that she was friend and that his boy used her phone sometimes. It was a lot of blah, blah, blah. I told him, "I'm not your girlfriend anymore; I am your wife. The cell phone had to go." So we went to counseling and discussed our problems, and he decided to leave the phone at the counseling session. For the next month, he didn't have a cell phone. It was hard for me also, because when he was gone I couldn't call him. But he started to call more often when he was out, to let me know when he'd be home and so forth. Everything was going good after this. We made it through the first year and three months, but after that he decided he wanted to leave the marriage. I remember that it was on a Good Friday. He felt that the marriage was too much pressure, and he didn't want a commitment anymore. He said he was trying to be something he couldn't be, even though he loved me. He said we rushed the marriage. I'm like, "*What!*" After three years in a relationship, you say we rushed into marriage?" We had known each other and were friends way before we started dating. "Come again please." I was totally lost and not knowing where all this was coming from. This was the worst news I had ever had to deal with. I felt like I was slowly dying. I told myself that maybe I wasn't a good enough wife, and I started blaming myself, even though I knew that he was the one with the real issues. I mean, we had been through hell and back, struggling together, and he wanted to wait till we were married to bail out? I felt like he had plenty of chances in our relationship to leave, and he didn't. Before we had even decided to get married, we had come clean about everything and anybody we had dealt with. Well, I found out later that I was the only one who was honest ... The separation is next!

SEPARATION

My husband told me how he felt on Friday April 18, 2003 (Good Friday). I don't know where everything came from, but it was not a good Friday for me; more like hell Friday. I believed we were doing well. There were no warning signs or anything. I felt like I didn't know this person anymore and that everything was just fake. I tried to stay mature about the situation; we talked over dinner and even made love three times that night. I had so many emotions going on that I didn't know which one to act on. I still loved my husband and thought we would honestly work it out. As he looked me in my face and told me he loved me but was not in love with me anymore, I just cried and said this is what happens sometimes. He proceeded to tell me how he had engaged in sexual activity with another girl but they did not have intercourse. I was in shock. I never suspected him of cheating on me. I still didn't want to lose my husband or my marriage. Unfortunately, there was not much I could do. He had made up his mind, and he didn't want any help and didn't want to be married anymore. As I think back I can now laugh, because everything was so stupid and I realize that a real man does not handle his business in that way. He just wanted to see other women and couldn't say it, so he used any excuse he could think of. People asked me if I would rather be in a marriage and have my husband cheat on me or just separate myself from the marriage. Back then I would have wanted to keep my marriage, but as I have become older and wiser, I think letting it go was the best thing to do. Not everybody is built for marriage, even if they think they are. He had so much he was trying to accomplish in his career, and I guess I was a hindrance—I don't know.

The marriage was gone, but our love for each other was still there. Due to the circumstances and having my heart pulled out we still associated with each other. When he left home I never took his key. We still made love together; we still did everything together. All his clothes were still at the house, but he wasn't. When he didn't take his clothes, I thought he would be back. But he never got a chance, because I had to move. I couldn't handle everything by myself. He had helped for one month with half of the rent, and that was it. I had to move back home with my parents. He left me with all the bills and everything, and at that time I was not working. I had left my job at the bank, because all the problems I was having were affecting my performance and my attendance. All he took were his clothes.

The pain I felt at not being with my husband on a daily basis was unbearable. I had so many hopes and dreams for our future and having a family together. It was everything we had talked about from day one. I thought we'd have kids together, and now it wasn't going to be a reality. I still prayed for my marriage and my husband. I let my emotions take me over, and I became violent at times and wanted revenge. I kept asking him why, and all he could say was, "I'm not in love with you" and "I don't want to be committed." I asked if it was about someone else, and he replied, "No!" Later I found out that it wasn't just about another girl, but other girls. I found out that he talked to a lot of girls but one in female in particular. I had to leave Buffalo for about three weeks because I thought I would end up in jail for killing or hurting somebody or even hurting myself. So I went to Charlotte to stay with my best friend just to clear my mind and get away from the home environment. I spoke to my husband a few times while I was away, and one night he told me he loved me before he hung up, and I was happy but also said to myself, "He doesn't love me enough to work out our marriage." Love had nothing to do with it anymore. When I returned home I was left to deal with reality once again. This time I dealt with the other woman, the same one I spoke to six months into the marriage, whose number was listed on the cell phone bill. I had a few arguments with this girl over the phone and had heard a lot of things on the street about her, but I didn't know what she looked like. I only knew what she drove.

One night I went to his house and I saw her car outside, so I went in the house. The downstairs door was locked, so I started using every key on my key chain. One of the keys worked, so I went in the house quietly till I reached upstairs, where the door was wide open. I went off as soon as I went in. Nothing was going on; she was just sitting on the couch. I remember looking at her dead in her face, and she moved to another couch. There was nothing she could possibly say or do; she remained silent. She couldn't leave, because I had blocked her car in the driveway. As I walked in I saw Allen and his two cousins in the kitchen cooking, so I went into the kitchen in a rage. They looked at me in disbelief, asking how I got in. They tried to grab me. I saw a knife on the table, and I picked it up and told them not to touch me. His cousin kept saying, "Tricey, chill out. Okay, put the knife down." I recall flipping the kitchen chairs over and everything. I put the knife down, and Allen and I started beefing. I had so much strength that night he could hardly control me. He kept trying to get me out of the house. I knew he wasn't going to hit me, but he did try to restrain me.

He had to drag me out of the house on my back while I was kicking him at the same time. He pushed me down the stairs, but I didn't fall. He kept saying, "We ain't together. You know our situation. I'm not with anybody. I'm just chilling." I told him, "I'm your wife still. You are still married, and you need to respect it." I was so hurt because he put me out and dragged me on the floor in front of his friends. I said, "Just file for divorce then and get it over with." I wanted to kill both of them that night. The girl never said anything to me. I think she was in shock and scared. He had to call my sister, and I called his sister and my friend Tysha to meet me over there. We tussled a little more outside; he kept trying to get me in my car, threatening to call the police on me. I didn't care; I wasn't going anywhere. My anger went from him to now wanting to get at her, but she wouldn't come outside. The same one who had so much mouth over the phone was speechless. Once my sister, his sister, and Tysha got there, it calmed down a little, but I still wasn't ready to leave. I eventually left and stayed the night at Tysha's house. I had brush burns on my damn back, and my eyes were heavy as hell from crying. That night was the worst. I kept trying to tell myself that I deserved much better, and I kept saying, "He is just a liar." He lied from the beginning, and she wasn't the only girl. My husband was becoming a ho! I believe if he would have been honest with me from the beginning a lot of this could have been avoided. There would be less pain and time I would have had to deal with. I was letting this destroy me, and I was tired of it. We stopped communication for about a month and tried to do the friend thing, but it just didn't work because of my feelings and emotions. I just knew too much about him that I didn't like. I had found out who the real Allen was. He wasn't the man I had married, and I didn't like or want Allen. So I decided to let everything go and just try to move on with my life. It was very hard; it took me a year to get over everything.

POETRY—THANKS

Thanks for showing me true love
when you did

Thanks for letting me experience
love and marriage
You gave me what no one else has
and I'll cherish it forever

Things may have not always worked out
But I enjoyed all the times they did
Memories last a lifetime

I have no regrets and I never will

May God give you peace and happiness

Take care, Babe!

DEPRESSION

I had never experienced depression until 2003. I always thought of myself as a strong person. I guess I fooled myself. There were days when I would stay in bed all day just crying, not eating. It's even hard for me to write this chapter without crying. There were days when I just wanted to take a bottle of aspirin and just die. I had no job, no husband, no money, and no hope. I felt like everything I lived for was gone, and what else was left? All the time and energy and all the sacrifices I had made in my life to better myself and my marriage were lost. I struggled to make us happy; when he didn't have it, I had it. I always did and still do want a child, and the thought of me not sharing that with my husband made me more depressed. I stopped going to church. Easter Sunday was the last Sunday I attended church; I dropped out of the choir and the praise team and turned in my secretary position. I was mad at church, at God and everyone. I felt all alone and felt that no one could help me, because I didn't want help. No one understood the pain that I was feeling. There was not a word of encouragement that anyone could say to make me feel better. I was partying heavily, going out three times a week, and I started back drinking alcohol all over again. This was a point in my life when I had really hit rock bottom. No one knew what I was going through. I no longer had a husband, I had lost my job, and I was living in a house that was not in the best of conditions. But I had to live there because my dad and I didn't get along. I didn't stay there too long because the water got turned off, so I had to move again. I was so down on money that I needed a way out. I decided to give dancing a try (strip). I remember telling Allen that I was going to do it because I had no other options at the time. He did not agree with it, but what else could I have done? My family didn't take care of me, and I only had myself to depend on. I told my mom and my sister, and they let me make my own decision. I went to two different locations to check it out, and then I decided one night to give it a try. My friend Tamara went with me; she was my support. I was so nervous. I had my three outfits and shoes, and I was ready to dance. I had to dance to three songs. I remember dancing to R. Kelly's "Move Your Body Like a Snake" and Christina Millian's "Dip it Low." I didn't have a problem once I got out on that stage. I actually had fun with it. I didn't make any money besides what my friend gave me. It was early on a weekday, so there was really no one in there. After that night, I decided that wasn't the life for me. They wanted me to dance, and the only way I could have made some real money was giving lap dances. I couldn't imagine going in a room with a complete stranger and dancing for him while he pays me money. I couldn't do it. So that never worked out for me. Once again I went back into a depression. I was drinking alcohol heavily, trying to drink away the pain, until ...

I saw a rainbow and just thought of butterflies and how I just wanted to fly and be beautiful and live. I got tired of crying and feeling sorry for myself. I gave up on God, and he had kept his hands on my life. I couldn't allow myself to die, especially not at the hands of a man. I just told myself that I have a purpose and I am a living testimony. I start saying I need to stick around to help other young females who might go through these things. The devil tried to kill and destroy me. So it was time to fight back. It's because of God's grace and mercy that I am still living.

I couldn't let any man dictate my future.

I couldn't let any problem make me feel like I wanted to die.

I couldn't let my circumstances dictate my future. I was going to have a future, with or without a husband. There is a reason for everything, and I believe it was a storm I had to go through and that it helped me become a better person. I'll be a good wife to someone, an excellent mother one day, or whatever else God puts in my life. Depression could not have a place in my life anymore. It was at this moment when I found a job and decided to go to hair school. It was still a struggle at times, but I did it and finished hair school successfully, and after that I went on and got my cosmetology license. I worked in a salon as an assistant for two years while living with a good friend of mine (Laura). This was the time in my life when I had the chance to get it together. While working at the salon I also went ahead and got my CDL so I could drive buses. Nothing could hold me back anymore, and I let all the past experiences go.

FINDING GOD

I grew up in the church. My grandmother (deceased) kept me grounded when it came to God. She was a praying grandmother. My cousins Jeanette and Mark (pastor and first lady now) would also take me and my brother to church with them on a regular basis. I never really experienced God for myself until I gave my life to Him in August 2000. I was on fire with God for two years straight. I didn't even think about going back to my worldly ways.

When I stayed away from God I didn't feel convicted, and that was not safe. I felt all alone and that he didn't care about me. I was twenty-four years old and dealing with a lot of issues. But then God spoke to me, and He said, "I could have let you die in your sin; I could have given you a child and had you raise the child on your own; I could have let you keep that man who wouldn't treat you like a queen. I didn't have to forgive you for your sins." I said thank you, because I would have gone straight to hell. *Mercy!*

It's because of God that I can love my enemies and pray for them. I'm still bitter toward one person, and God is still working on me in that area; I don't know when I will forgive or pray for that enemy. I can't forgive or forget. It's because of God that I can forgive my husband. It's because of God that I am free from bondage—the chains are gone. I can praise him through my pain. I am wiser, stronger, and a better women. I owe it all to God. Thank you!

JESUS,

YOU'RE THE CENTER OF MY JOY

When I feel I'm down and my back's against the wall
You are my Center

When my friends are gone and family doesn't care at all
You are my Center

When I feel like dying and leaving this world
You are my Center

When my husband left me and I felt all hope was gone
You were my Center

When I'm all alone and have nothing to call my own
You are my Center

When no one cares
And the pain is too hard to bear
You are my Center.

EXHALING

I'm free. I am striving to be whatever God is calling me to be. I have exhaled, and I'm breathing fresh air. I am that beautiful butterfly. As I end my autobiography, I will inform you that my husband and I are still currently legally married. I am taking care of myself. I've always focused on everyone else, and now I'm focusing on me.

UPDATE: This autobiography was written in 2003–2004, with the intention of having it published and in your hands by 2005, but it didn't work out that way, so I had to add another chapter, titled Divorce. Read on …

Even when the love is gone, it's always good to try to remain friends. We were friends before we were a couple, so to keep everything peaceful we are trying to remain friends. Sometimes we don't get along, and it's okay; everything is not always going to be sweet. It's hard to be a friend to someone you love or once loved. The hardest part for me was letting go. A lot of people can only let go if they don't deal with the other person at all. I had to try to let go and still try to keep a friendship with him. There were plenty of times when I let my feelings and emotions get in the way, but I learned how to deal with them and pull away when I needed to.

Now I have to learn how to deal with the other person (girl). What we had is over, so it's time for us both to move on. Seeing the person that you once shared your life with with someone else hurts, but you will survive. We are currently in the process of making the divorce official, and we are trying to stay mature about the situation so that it's not a nasty divorce. I don't have all the answers, but God is helping me in the areas that I am still struggling with.

DIVORCE

Divorce is something that I never thought I would have had to experience. I mean, even with all the problems that go along with marriage you always want to bet the odds and work it out and not end in divorce.

The odds were against me, and I decided to file for divorce on February 16, 2005. Allen and I had talked and decided that it was the best thing to do, and he agreed to pay for it. He had apologized, and I forgave him. We talked about everything and just remained really good friends. I didn't want to be separated forever and never get back together, and I didn't want to still be married and dating other people. While we were separated, we still continued to see each other on and off. We still loved and cared for each other, and to this day I still love and care for him.

After I filed, I questioned myself over and over: did I make the right decision? Yes, because that same week, Allen had come over to my house to talk to me. He was being really silly, and when I said, "What?" he kept saying, "I don't know how to tell you this." When he said that I knew what he was talking about, and I asked him before he could even tell me. I said, "You got somebody pregnant?"

and he said, "Yeah." My next question was, "Who?" and he said the girl's name. Well, I didn't know this girl, so that was good, because if it had been one of the drama girls, I would have been really mad. I knew he wasn't ready for kids, so I asked him what he was going to do. He told me that she was keeping it because she wouldn't have an abortion. I understood that, because I would never have one either, no matter what. He told me that the girl was scared of what I would say and how I would react, and I told him, "That is your life now; we are basically over as far as the marriage is concerned." So I was cool with it, because it was better her than me. I wasn't ready for kids, especially not with him at that time. I remember that on that same night I talked to his mom and his sisters, and they all wanted to make sure I was okay. His mom always wanted me to give her another grandchild.

I had always wanted a family with Allen and desired a child for the longest time, but it wasn't meant for us. What was meant for us had happened already, and it was fun while it lasted. (I later found out that I couldn't have kids anyway.)

Confirmation: On February 23, 2005, when I came home from work, I found a big envelope. When I opened it, I found my divorce papers. The divorce was final. But the ironic thing about it was that February 23 was the same date we had got married on, three years prior. I said, "Wow, what a confirmation—the date it started and the date it ended." I ran upstairs to my sister's house and did a happy dance. I then called Al and said, "Happy Anniversary; it's final," and he said, "What?" I said, "The divorce." He had his papers and didn't even know what they were. It just seemed like I was finally free; he could go on with his life and I could go on with mine.

People never will understand to this day what we shared, and what we did share can never be replaced, no matter how hard we try. The divorce ended our marriage, but it did not end our friendship or the way I still feel about him. For a while we would still mess around with each other occasionally, but that ended in 2005 when his daughter was born. I haven't looked back since. I would still find myself having to argue with the silly girls from the past, because people did not want us to be friends and couldn't get over it. We (me and Allen) are friends forever, from the same hood for life.

People have choices, and we made the right choices so we could go on with our individual lives. People still can't believe that we never got back together, and every time I see someone, they always ask me how he is doing. I say he is doing just fine!

FYI: After all we went through I still and always will love that boy, and that's *final.*

POETRY

I WISH

I wish that you didn't have to leave
meaning I want you to stay
Lie with me, hold me, and keep the lonely away
Relax as we kiss the night away
Your touch is what I need
Your air is what I breathe
If only for one night
We can sleep the night away
You and me
As we lay
I wish

YOU DON'T KNOW ME

When you left me
I didn't know what to do
You left me so confused
What used to be home
Was no longer home
We were once so much in love
I thought you were an angel sent from above
But like Brandy said, "You were an angel in disguise"
How do I know, you ask? I saw it with my own eyes
I don't deserve to be treated like a fool or treated so cruel
I won't do it anymore, so when you return to what once was our

home
Pack your bags and get gone
I'd rather be alone than be with you
Heartbreak, I can't do
If you can't be true then we can't be
So like the famous T. I. said
"When you see me in the streets, remember you don't know me!"

THANKFUL

I lie awake at night
Thinking about you
Wondering where you are
What you're thinking
And do you love me

It's hard to sleep
Always thinking thoughts so deep
Never have I had someone
As special as you

Every day looking to the sky
Asking God am I deserving of you
Maybe enough pain was given to me
That happiness comes through you

Love conquers everything, and
Your love has conquered me

Thanks for setting me free

SISTAS

Why do we put up with so much?
Are we weak?
Is it because we don't know our worth?
Is it because we are lonely or stupid?
Why do we settle?
Is it low self-esteem?
Or because the bills are being paid?
Is it because you think you can't do better?
Or do you let your hormones take over?

We are beautiful
We are precious
We are worth more than diamonds
We are successful
We are good mothers
We are good wives
We can make it
We are not cheap; we are not punching bags
We are women
Be wise

Why do we put up with so much?
Ask yourself and then answer
If you answer yourself, then work on changing yourself, because you
shouldn't put up with so much. Be strong and be a real SISTA!

DO YOU REMEMBER?

Do you remember the first time coming to my house?
Do you remember the first time we went out?
Do you remember buttoning my coat?
Do you remember holding my through the night?
Do you remember our first kiss?
Do you remember our first dance?
Do you remember holding hands?
Do you remember the first time we made love?
Do you remember my favorite song?
Do you remember looking in my eyes?
Do you remember the first time I cried?
Do you remember saying I love you?
Do you remember you saying, "I don't deserve you"?
Do you remember the first time you tasted my love?
Do you remember the first time I tasted your love?
Do you remember our first 69?
Do you remember all these good times?
Do you remember saying I do?
Do you remember me smiling at you?
Do you remember all of our ups and downs?
Do you remember promising me you'd stay around?
Do you remember saying you don't want a marriage?
Do you remember silence?
Do you remember hearing my heart hit the floor?
Do you remember if I ever picked it back up?
Do you? Do you remember?

LOSING YOU

When I lost you, I was very young
When I lost you, I felt like a woman
When I lost you, I became free
When I lost you, I didn't cry
When I lost you, I was high
When I lost you, you got attention
When I lost you, I mistreated you
When I lost you, I let people take
      advantage of you
I let people abuse you
I let diseases attack you
I apologize, now when it's too late. If I could turn back the hands
of time, I'd still have you.

Don't lose me until you're ready, physically, emotionally, mentally,
and married.
     Signed: Virginity

MY ENCOURAGEMENT

"Why" is the question I keep asking
"I don't understand" is what I keep saying
When will I find true happiness?
Relationships and a marriage and guess what
I'm still hurt
I'm still crying
I still have pain
Every man in my life has let me down
My heart is still broken
"Why" I tried to do my best and it wasn't enough

Now I'm trying something different
Do me
Appreciate me
I am a queen
I am beautiful
I am a jewel
I am that beautiful butterfly

I am a better person because of my
journey and life experiences. Nothing else will hurt me. I've been
through it all—pain, lies, betrayal, adultery, fighting, arguing, tears,
depression, abuse (mentally and physically), and I lost my self.

No more drama is allowed in my life

THANK YOU

First and foremost I thank my heavenly father for his grace and mercy. Thank you for keeping your hands on my life. Thanks to my mom and dad for producing a wonderful, beautiful individual (smile). Mom, words can't express my gratitude for you, and I thank you for always being supportive of anything I did; you never once judged me. Dad, I love you and thank you for all the times when you didn't turn your back on me when I had nowhere else to go, even when we were beefing. To my sister Michelle, thanks for always believing in me. To my other siblings (Anthony [my heart], Jackie, Freeman, Janice, Tony, Linda, and Albert), I love y'all.

To Johnal, thanks for showing me real love and loving me when you did and giving me memories for a lifetime. I will always love you for that.

To my pastor and first lady Hennings, thank you for always keeping me encouraged with your sweet words, and thank you for keeping your doors open for counseling; without your help and God I don't know where I'd be. To the Zion Dominion family, thank you for all your prayers and love.

Thanks to the Gleen family for always accepting me and loving me as your own—love y'all. To Mommy Byrd, you're still my second mommy, and I couldn't ask for a better mother-in-law. To my sisters Tomea and Sugar, thanks for everything. Tomea, you have overcome so much in your life, and I will always be here for you.

To all my nieces and nephews, Auntie T. T. loves y'all, and y'all are my true inspirations!

To Mike (RIP), your death has made me realize that there's more to life than drama; you are indeed a hero. To Monique, thanks for being my friend always. We have shared our ups and downs together and got through them together. We are going to get our mansion one day (I made it, Gyrl), and don't forget that we are the first ladies of OTB.

To Tysha, thanks for always giving me your shoulder to cry on and being there continuously even when I felt like I didn't want to be there myself. You were there every step of the way. I'm all right now. We have a bond that can't be replaced.

To Laura, thanks for listening and talking to me when I needed you and sharing your home with me.

Hey Angie, I didn't forget ya. I remember how we met (through God/Minnie). You have been a great friend, and I hope this inspires you to write your story, Love ya!

To Santoshia, my new found friend. There has been nothing but love, support, and encouragement between us since day one. I appreciate you, and so does your adopted niece (Niah)!

To my friends for life—Javaughn (BF since pre-k), Tamara, Rhonda, and Keyta—we still get hated on: "The crew they love to hate." We are 5*. There is not a chapter I could have written to explain our friendship. I would need another book for that. We have been through everything together. We are the meaning of "friendship." We have grown together, laughed together, cried together, prayed together, and fought together, and for some of us we have lived together. I don't know what life would be like without you girls! You all have loved, supported, and encouraged me and have always stood right by my side. There are no rights or wrongs with us; it's just love. I love y'all. God couldn't have given me any better friends for a lifetime! Twenty-plus years ... Wow!

To my Smile 4 me :). I did it. "Who but me"! Nothing but love! I got a thang for you!

To my cuz Dae, thanks for always keeping me informed and being my number-one cousin. To my cousin Tika, thank you for everything. You were there for me along my journey as well. To the Ill block, love y'all. Thanks for teaching me the streets. To my GYC (492) family, I know where I am from and will represent at all times! To everybody on Moselle St., I couldn't have been raised on any other street. We had good times!

To my Facebook friends, continue to support me. I appreciate all the love!

To my new family, my Jazzy's crew: Jordache, Char, Delores, Fee, Bear, Tamara, Dion, and Tonya. (We gets it in.)

To my family who has adopted me as their sister—Fam (Dodee), Yayo (Bear), and L. L. (Jeff)—as long as I got my front, I always know y'all will have my back! To Bookey, you are a great person, and I wish you nothing but happiness. Thanks for being my friend and always encouraging me to do better.

To the Brooks and Taylor families, I love y'all. To all my uncles (Gus, Charles, Thadford, Carl), I love y'all. To my uncle Thadford, I want to say thank you for always being there to lend a helping hand to me when no one else's hand was available. I will always appreciate everything you did, because there were times when I didn't know how I would make it.

To all my friends and family; there are too many to name. Thank you for everything you have ever done for me, and continue to support and pray for me.

To Mario, my friend, my brother, you are missed and will never be forgotten. I told you I was going to stay out of trouble and "do me." Thanks for always listening and understanding me and never taking sides. Rest in peace!

To my grandparents, Gus D. Brooks Sr. and Luella Brooks, even though you are no longer here to share in my success and to read my story, I am sure you are sitting beside "Him" looking down on me smiling, and I know you will continue to protect me. RIP and I miss you so much! Until we meet again.

Thank you for your support of my first autobiography
The sky is the limit … This is the *good life*.

Life is not always easy, life is not always nice, life is not always fair, but life is life, and while you are breathing and here on this earth, enjoy life to the fullest and make the best out of what you have in life.

I would like to thank God for giving me the strength and courage to write my book. Without his grace and mercy I would not be here. I would not be able to share my experiences and all of my downfalls with you if it weren't for him. I am a new person now, wiser and stronger as a *woman*. As women we need to step up our game. This is our year; well, at least it's *my year!* This book is to encourage you so that you will be *wise women*.

I don't have all the answers, and I struggle in some areas of my life. I am not perfect, but I am trying to better myself and my surroundings. If I have hurt anyone in any way, shape, or form, this is my apology, because life is too short and we as a people need to build on love and not hate. Buffalo is full of negativity and hate. Let's do better for the sake of our children; we have to be good examples.

I have already started writing my second book, so be on the lookout
for it to be available soon.
God bless and *live*.

Ms. Tricey219

My Journey

MY JOURNEY CONTINUES.

Manufactured By: RR Donnelley
Breinigsville, PA USA
July, 2010